Your Great State

by Daphne Liu

Illustrated by Amanda Haley

HAMPTON-BROWN

9:00 A.M.
Meet at School

The day is finally here! Our class is going to the State Capitol. We have to learn about state government. I wish we could go to the zoo or the science museum instead! I mean, what's so great about state government?

Ms. Reyes says our school gets a lot of money from the state. Without that money, we might not be able to go on ANY field trips. Hmmm. . . I never thought about that before!

our teacher, Ms. Reyes

our driver, Mr. Mike

The state helped pay for this bus.

SCHOOL BUS

our bus

How the State Helps Schools:

✔ pays for books, computers, and other supplies

✔ helps pay for school lunches

✔ decides what students need to learn

✔ gives tests to see what students learned

✔ decides the number of days in the school year

9:30 A.M.
On the Road

There are orange plastic cones all over this highway! Workers are fixing holes in the road and making the road wider. This will make a lot more room for cars. Other workers are picking up trash. This will make the road a lot more beautiful!

Ms. Reyes says that the state builds new highways and fixes old ones, so people can get around our great state!

on State Highway 68

10:30 A.M.
Hello, University!

We just passed the state university. Ms. Reyes went to this college a long, long, LONG time ago! She says that the state helped pay for her college education. The state gives money to universities, so universities don't need as much money from students. Then it doesn't cost as much to go to college.

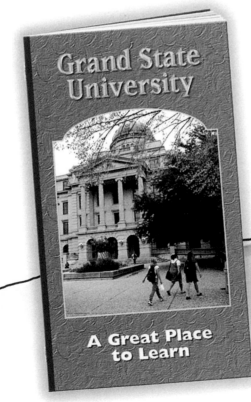

Grand State University

A Great Place to Learn

students at
Grand State University

11:30 A.M.
Lunchtime

This park is a perfect place for lunch. I'm glad, because I'm ready to eat!

The park ranger just introduced herself to us. She explained that the state has many parks. The state pays rangers like her to protect the people, plants, and animals in the parks. The state keeps all the parks clean and safe so everyone can enjoy the great outdoors!

Greetings from
Blackhawk State Park

1:00 P.M.
Stuck in Traffic!

I can't believe it! We have been on the highway for 30 minutes, and we have not moved! Everyone is getting very upset—especially our bus driver. I don't think he likes being stuck in traffic with 23 kids, four parents and one tired teacher.

1:15 P.M.
Still Waiting...

A police officer told us what's wrong. There was an accident, and now the road is blocked. We have to wait for a truck to tow away the cars that were in the accident.

Ms. Reyes says that the state has police officers called troopers. They help people on the highway. They also make sure drivers obey the law.

Trooper Evans

check how fast people are driving

help people in accidents

What State Troopers Do

watch for trouble on the roads

give directions to people who are lost

1:30 P.M.
Out of the Way!

We're finally moving again. An ambulance just drove by. Its siren was loud! Mr. Mike had to stop and let the ambulance pass. It's taking someone to the hospital.

Ms. Reyes says that the state owns some hospitals. The state also makes sure that doctors and nurses know how to do their jobs. They must go to special classes and pass a lot of tests before they are allowed to work in a hospital in this state.

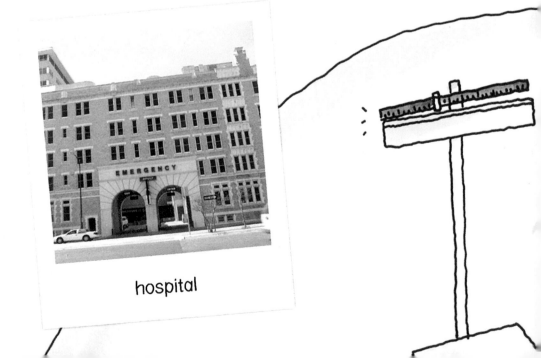

hospital

1:45 P.M.
Over the Bridge

Why did we have to pay money to cross this bridge? It's only a short drive to the other side!

Ms. Reyes says that the state owns some roads and bridges. Sometimes we have to pay to drive on them. The money helps the state take care of the roads and bridges.

Awesome view!

2:00 P.M.
We're Here!

Finally, we're at the State Capitol! This is where our state leaders work. I can't wait to go inside and look around.

What a big building! I guess that's because our state leaders have a big job. They give us schools, parks, roads, bridges, hospitals, and a lot of other things that help make our state GREAT!

Huge dome!

State Capitol